A Knife *and a* Fork
and a Bottle
and a Cork

That's How You Spell
New York

RIDDLE RHYME
1
TRILOGY

Requests for permission should be addressed to:

LEMONTREE PRESS
P.O. Box 841
Santa Cruz, California 95061

Printed in China

Copyright © 2010 Howard Schrager
First Printed Edition (the "Xerox Special") 1994
ISBN-13: 978-0-9644846-3-4
ISBN-10: 0-9644846-3-3

A Knife *and a* Fork
and a Bottle
and a Cork

That's How You Spell
New York

Riddle Rhymes by Howard Schrager
Illustrations by Sarah Madsen

Happy Riddle Rhymes!

PUBLISHED BY

Lemon Tree Press

DEDICATIONS

*For my father, the late Julius Schrager, who taught me Riddle Rhymes,
and who gave me so much more than I will ever know.*
H.S.

For my dear family and friends who always believe in me.
Love and smiles always,
S.M.

ACKNOWLEDGMENTS and THANKS

First of all I want to acknowledge the Santa Cruz Waldorf School Class of 1994, all grown up now, for working with me, especially on the original illustrations. They are: Jonna Anderson, Amanda Brugioni, Claire Cunliffe, Paul Dembowski, Daphne Descollanges, Genevieve Dobbins, Katya Hurwitz, Cameron Kelly, Eva Nagel, Eve Newman, Lilia Webber, and Jeremy Williams.

I also wish to thank Shan Kendall, Anita Warren, Stephen Spitalny, Leah Rubin, and Gayle and Alan Williams for their participation in creating the first edition. Thanks, too, to Ashok Shevde, Tori Milburn, Suni Gibbons, and the late James Staffen for their help in its production. Also, particular thanks to my old friend, Richard Paris, for suggesting the name 'Riddle Rhyme'.

A very large thank you to Sarah Madsen, my illustrator, who has brought such heart and imagination to the illustrations, working under anything but optimal conditions. She is sensational!

Special thanks to my former student, Soren McVay, SCWS Class of 2004, for her fine editorial work.

Finally, thanks to Toni Henderson, for her continual support, and for her discernment, and overall good sense.

PREFACE

A number of years ago I was watching the movie, *Cinema Paradiso*, when it cut to a scene of a hen roosting in an abandoned car. Suddenly, the words of a street rhyme my father had taught me when I was seven, from his own childhood in the 1920s, came to mind, "Chicken in the Car and the Car Can't Go, that's how you spell CHICAGO". I recalled, too, that there was a companion rhyme to the first that went, "A Knife and a Fork and a Bottle and a Cork, that's how you spell NEW YORK". For me there was no question that, in its particular way, this was how to "spell" these places. It was magical, and fun!

Not long after my *Cinema Paradiso* experience, I thought, "Why not create a Riddle Rhyme for each of the 50 states, and perhaps, the cities, too." At the time my 8th grade class at the Santa Cruz Waldorf School was looking to earn money for their end-of-year trip, so I brought the idea to them. While, for the most part, they had a hard time wrapping their minds around writing Riddle Rhymes, they did eagerly take on illustrating the ones I had written. We published a "Xerox special", entitled A Knife and A Fork and Bottle and a Cork, which was enjoyed by those in our circle of friends and neighbors, and it did help get us where we were going.

Over the years I have revised some of the Riddle Rhymes, and written new ones, for the major cities and the state capitals. I have also asked the wonderfully imaginative and whimsical artist, Sarah Madsen, to illustrate the Riddle Rhymes in her inimitable style.

I have always enjoyed watching people guess these Riddle Rhymes. I have observed that a deeper thought process is going on than one might at first imagine. A different type of logic is at work, or, at play. Guessing Riddle Rhymes is not like playing *Jeopardy*. There is not a specific fact that one knows or doesn't know, which must be answered before an opponent does. Rather, there is a quasi- poetic process occurring, which entails listening, then hearing, while an inner sifting takes place, and the words of the rhymes resonate with the name of a familiar state. It is a very special, and a very sociable, process.

My job is to lead and mislead at the same time, to lead you onto the right path, and to throw you off the track a bit. While the apparent object of doing Riddle Rhymes is to guess the state, I hope you will find that there is much more to it than that.

You will find that Riddle Rhymes make a wonderful travel game, ice-breaker, fireside activity, or unique and entertaining way of bringing U.S. Geography into the classroom, at any level. This unique form of "spelling" will generate joy and enthusiasm. Guaranteed.

Good Luck, and Happy Riddle Rhyming,

Howard Schrager

MONTEREY, CA
August 2009

How To Do Riddle Rhymes

1. The object of this activity is to answer the riddle suggested by the rhyme, or verse. The answer to the riddle is the name of one of the 50 states.

2. The answer to the riddle is "wrapped up" in the words and sounds of the rhyme, or verse. Your job is to unwrap it.

3. Riddle Rhymes work best when read aloud in a group. The sounds contained in the words of the rhymes suggest the name of a state; they don't actually spell it , in the usual sense of 'spelling'. Let's say the riddle is something like a 'magic spell', and that you need to break the spell.

4. All of the sounds in the verse do not have to do with the name of the state. Some are there to throw you off, or to hide the answer, or just to make the riddle a little better.

5. The rhythm of the verse, too, helps reveal the answer. Rhythm has to do with the number of syllables, and where the accent is placed. Two states with different rhythms, for example, would be Minnesota and Texas, or Maine and Utah. Nevada and Hawaii would be similar.

6. It is important to say, "that's how you spell". It calls the question. It helps you to take the leap off the diving board. Maybe it gets you out of the left side of your brain. Therefore, don't say, "I'm a left brain type person." Try a few first. Don't give up.

7. Never look up an answer to a Riddle Rhyme (pg. 51), unless you are desperate. Rather, go on to another one and come back to it later. Just by trying, you have gotten part way to the answer.

8. Listen to the others who are guessing along with you. They will often give you clues as they home in on the correct response.

9. What do you do once you have guessed them all? This can be the best part. Now the pressure is off. Bring Riddle Rhymes to others and watch how the mind works.

10. Before you begin guessing, read the STATES BY HEART (page 58). This will ensure that the names are fresh in your mind.

Table of Contents

Noah built the ark
with a hammer and saw.

That's how you spell...

"Paper or plastic?"
they always ask ya.

That's how you spell...

Glue can connect,
and a scissors can cut.

That's how you spell...

Bones, bones in the arid zones; and no one can find the owner.

That's how you spell...

Ten cents tax to step on the bus.

That's how you spell...

It's hard to eat cold, hard dough.

That's how you spell...

A week's worth of washing
musta' weighed a ton.

That's how you spell...

Down by the flowing river, la dee dah –

That's how you spell...

Next week, two months ago –

That's how you spell...

How to swim?
Why to ski?

That's how you spell...

Maintain your sun tan, Hanna.

That's how you spell...

Silly boys make lots of noise.

That's how you spell...

Mayonnaise mixed with rain.

That's <u>mainly</u> how you spell...

Corn bread with four eggs on –

That's how you spell...

**Lou went down
   to see his Aunt Anna.**

That's how you spell...

Mary had a little land.

That's how you spell...

**Monkey's missing from the zoo;
it's a mystery.**

That's how you spell...

Never break eggs into a grass basket.

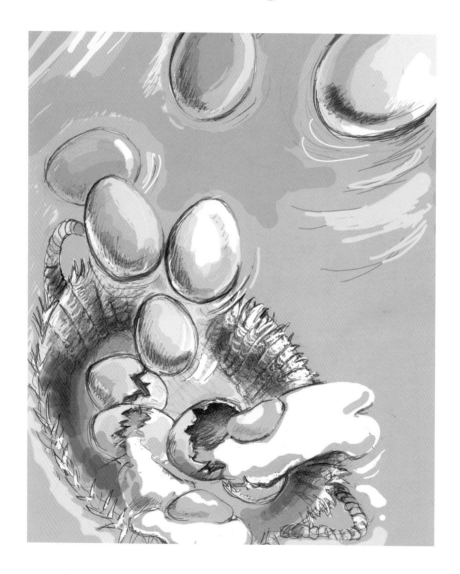

That's how you spell...

A knife and a fork and
a bottle and a cork –

That's how you spell...

Sue is sure
she wants a new hamster.

That's how you spell...

You grew your tulips too tall!

That's how you spell...

Verymuchmany
is a great amount.

That's how you spell...

An oak fulla' acorns
backa' ma' home –

That's how you spell...

Whiskey mixed in
the cotton gin –

That's how you spell...

On earth cars are all lined up.

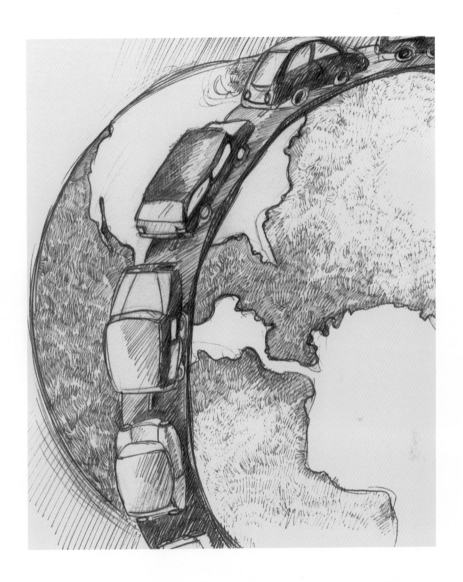

That's how you spell...

Sore throat?
Keep the coat on.

That's how you spell...

A mass of massive
gum chewing bassets –

That's how you spell...

Railroad to Ireland
runs through Thailand.

That's how you spell...

Who knows
what's best for Junior?

That's how you spell...

Out of the wilds rode
the old gnome king.

That's how you spell...

The navy crew wore
blue shirt sleeves.

That's how you spell...

My sister married a hippy.

That's how you spell...

Succotash with carrots
over rice on china –

That's how you spell...

Mini-marts
sell many sodas.

That's how you spell...

Go as high as you can go!

That's how you spell...

Oh, no, missed again!

That's how you spell...

Furniture for pigeons –

That's how you spell...

The hen and the ducky
got real lucky!

That's how you spell...

Can you can a can of sauce?

That's how you spell...

I know a secret, ha ha ha!

That's how you spell...

Too much gum
　　jams George's jaw.

That's how you spell...

I'd use a hoe
if the tractor wouldn't go.

That's how you spell...

Lost my love;
never had her.

That's how you spell...

Ten tents by the sea –

That's how you spell...

Too far to go,
not to go to.

That's how you spell...

Delicious fruit, the apple
and pear –

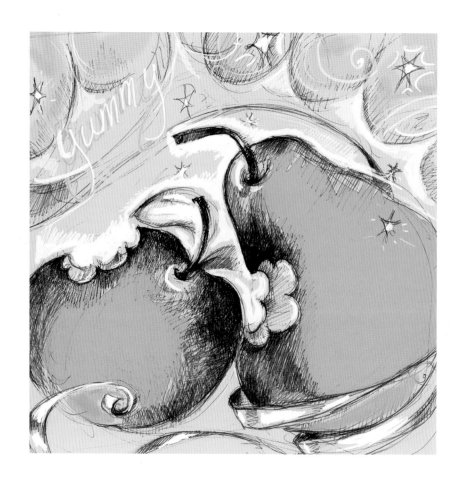

That's how you spell...

Fence on the hill
at the end of the lane –

<u>Yeah</u>, that's how you spell...

Cauliflower, corn and
peas are good for ya'.

That's how you spell...

Al ate a sandwich of ham and banana.

That's how you spell...

In the end
a white bandanna –

That's how you spell...

ANSWERS by page number

1. Arkansas
2. Alaska
3. Connecticut
4. Arizona
5. Texas
6. Colorado
7. Washington
8. Florida
9. New Mexico
10. Hawaii
11. Montana
12. Illinois
13. Maine
14. Oregon
15. Louisiana
16. Maryland
17. Missouri
18. Nebraska
19. New York
20. New Hampshire
21. Utah
22. Vermont
23. Oklahoma
24. Wisconsin
25. North Carolina

26. South Dakota
27. Massachusetts
28. Rhode Island
29. West Virginia
30. Wyoming
31. New Jersey
32. Mississippi
33. South Carolina
34. Minnesota
35. Ohio
36. Michigan
37. Virginia
38. Kentucky
39. Kansas
40. Iowa
41. Georgia
42. Idaho
43. Nevada
44. Tennessee
45. North Dakota
46. Delaware
47. Pennsylvania
48. California
49. Alabama
50. Indiana

THE 50 STATES

STATE	CAPITAL	NAME ORIGIN
Alabama	Montgomery	(Alabama Indians). 'I clear the thicket.'
Alaska	Juneau	(Aleut), 'mainland', 'land that is not an island'.
Arizona	Phoenix	(Pima) name of village *Arizona*, near Nogales, AZ ...'place of the small spring' / (Basque) 'good oak'
Arkansas	Little Rock	(Quapaw Indians) 'downstream people'
California	Sacramento	named after fictional island, *Califia*, described around 1500 by Garci Ordonez de Montalvo
Connecticut	Hartford	(Algonquin) 'long tidal river', after Connecticut River
Delaware	Dover	from Thomas West, Baron de la Warr, first governor of Virginia
Florida	Tallahassee	(Spanish) 'full of flowers'
Georgia	Atlanta	from King George II of England who granted charter to James Oglethorpe in 1733
Hawaii	Honolulu	*Ava-iki*, 'the bright land of Vatea', 'ancestral home'
Idaho	Boise	(Comanche) Ida = salmon, Ho = tribe or (Shoshone) ee-da-how 'Behold! The sun is coming down the mountain'
Illinois	Springfield	(Illiniweck) 'perfect man'
Indiana	Indianapolis	'Land of the Indians'
Iowa	Des Moines	(Sioux) 'sleepy ones', *Ayuwah* name given to area tribe by Sioux enemies
Kansas	Topeka	(Sioux) 'people of the south wind'
Kentucky	Frankfort	(Cherokee) *Ken-tah-ke*, 'prairie' or 'meadowland'
Louisiana	Baton Rouge	named for King Louis XIV of France, *Louisiane* by Robert Cavelier de La Salle in 1682
Maine	Augusta	early explorers called it 'The Main' to distinguish it from offshore islands
Maryland	Annapolis	for Queen Henrietta Maria, wife of Charles I of England, 1634
Massachusetts	Boston	(Algonquin) 'near the great hill'
Michigan	Lansing	(Algonquin) michi = large, gami = lake
Minnesota	St. Paul	(Sioux) after the longest river within its boundaries, name means 'clouded water' because of silty appearance

Mississippi	Jackson	(Algonquin) 'father of waters'
Missouri	Jefferson City	(Algonquin) 'people with big canoes'
Montana	Helena	(Spanish) 'mountainous region'
Nebraska	Lincoln	(Oto) Nebrathka, meaning 'flat water' after Platte River
Nevada	Carson City	(Spanish) 'snow-covered'
New Hampshire	Concord	after Hampshire, England
New Jersey	Trenton	after Jersey in the Channel Islands
New Mexico	Santa Fe	to distinguish it from nation to the south
New York	Albany	after Duke of York, later King James II of England
North Carolina	Raleigh	after Charles I of England
North Dakota	Bismarck	(Sioux) 'allies'
Ohio	Columbus	(Iroquois) 'large creek'
Oklahoma	Oklahoma City	(Choctaw) 'red man'; Okla = people, homa = red
Oregon	Salem	(uncertain) perhaps (Fr) 'hurricane'
Pennsylvania	Harrisburg	*Penn's Woods*; named by Charles II of England after Admiral William Penn, father of William Penn, founder of the colony
Rhode Island	Providence	(Dutch) roodt eylandt, 'red island', referring to Aquidneck Island
South Carolina	Columbia	after Charles II of England who granted 'Carolina' in 1663
South Dakota	Pierre	(Sioux) 'alliance of friends'
Tennessee	Nashville	(unknown) named for Tinasi, a Cherokee village, meaning unknown
Texas	Austin	(Spanish + Indian) tejas, techas, meaning 'friends' or 'allies'
Utah	Salt Lake City	(Apache) 'high'; Mormon name Deseret, meaning 'honeybee', signifying industriousness
Vermont	Montpelier	(French) 'green mountain'
Virginia	Richmond	after Queen Elizabeth I, the 'Virgin Queen', i.e. never married
Washington	Olympia	named in honor of our first president
West Virginia	Charleston	at outset of Civil War voted for separation from Virginia; was first to be named Kanhawa
Wisconsin	Madison	(Ojibwa) 'gathering of waters' after its principal river
Wyoming	Cheyenne	(Delaware) 'at the big river flat'; name transplanted westward from Wyoming Valley in Pennsylvania

BODY GEOGRAPHY

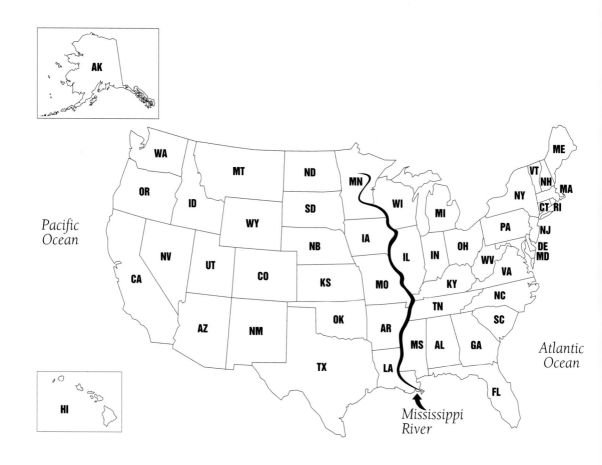

AK

WA
MT
ND
MN
OR
ID
SD
WI
ME
VT
NH
MA
NY
CT RI
WY
NB
IA
MI
PA
NJ
Pacific
Ocean
NV
UT
CO
IL
IN
OH
WV
DE
MD
CA
KS
MO
KY
VA
AZ
NM
OK
AR
TN
NC
SC
MS
AL
GA
Atlantic
Ocean
TX
LA
FL

HI

Mississippi
River

IMAGINE your upper body as a map of the United States:

Your <u>waist</u> is the southern boundary (more or less).

Your <u>shoulders</u> are the northern boundary.

Your <u>right arm</u> outstretched to the side touches northern California.

Your <u>left arm</u> outstretched touches Maryland.

The <u>midline of your body</u> is the Mississippi River. *We can have it this way, even though only 1/3 of the lands lie east of the Mississippi, because so many states and so much population is concentrated in the east.*

TO DO Body Geography

Move the appropriate hand to the body location that best represents the place on the map. For example:

Maine	<u>Left hand</u> fully extended slightly above shoulder level
Florida	<u>Left hand</u> fully extended slightly below waist
Washington	<u>Right hand</u> fully extended at shoulder level
Montana	<u>Right hand</u> near shoulder in 'push up' position
Minnesota	<u>Right hand</u> at shouder level at midline
Ohio	<u>Left hand</u> in 'push up' position.
Mississippi	<u>Left hand</u> slightly left of belly button
Louisiana	<u>Right hand</u> slightly right of belly button
Oklahoma	<u>Right hand</u> at lowest rib
etc.	These are approximate positions. Work them out for yourself.

The ULTIMATE

Use a wall map and a pointer, or yardstick. Establish a tempo you are comfortable with, using a metronome, or an inner one, by tapping your foot. Begin reciting the states in order, or have someone read them to you (which is harder), while pointing to each state in turn. There can be no pauses, if one is to succeed in passing this ultimate test.

One Fact Per State

1. **Alabama** is the home of two of the greatest baseball players of all time, Willie Mays and Hank Aaron.
2. **Alaska** has more miles of coastline than all the other states together.
3. **Arizona** was the last state admitted (1912) before Hawaii and Alaska (1959).
4. The only diamond mine in North America is found in **Arkansas**.
5. The highest point (Mt. Whitney 14,495 ft.), and the lowest point (Bad Water, in Death Valley, 280 ft. below sea level), lie within 100 mi. of each other, in Mono County, **California**.
6. **Colorado** contains 75% of land area in the U.S. with altitude above 10,000ft.
7. **Connecticut** has the highest income per capita of any state.
8. **Delaware**, the second smallest state, was the first to ratify the Constitution.
9. **Florida** is not the southernmost state; Hawaii is.
10. **Georgia** is the largest state east of the Mississippi River, in terms of land area.
11. **Hawaii's** Mt. Waialeale is the wettest place on earth, with 460 in. of rainfall annually.
12. **Idaho** produces 72 types of precious and semi-precious stones, some of which can be found nowhere else, which is why it is known as the "Gem State".
13. **Illinois** is known for its wide variety of weather, major winter storms, tornadoes, and severe heat and cold waves.
14. More major highways intersect in **Indiana** than in any other state.
15. **Iowa** is the only state bounded by two rivers that ships can navigate, the Mississippi and the Missouri.
16. **Kansas** wheat farmers produced enough wheat in 1990 to make 33 billion loaves of bread, 6 loaves for every person in the world.
17. **Kentucky** was the first state west of the Appalachian Mountains.
18. **Louisiana** is the only state with a large population of Cajuns, descendants of the Acadians, who were driven out of Canada in the 1700's because they would not pledge allegiance to the King of England.
19. **Maine** is the only state that borders only one other state. (New Hampshire).
20. From 1763 to 1767, Charles Mason and Jeremiah Dixon surveyed **Maryland's** northern boundary with Pennsylvania. This came to be called the Mason-Dixon Line.
21. **Massachusetts** is called the 'Cradle of Liberty', because it was the center for the movement for independence from Great Britain. The first shots of the Revolutionary War were fired at Lexington.
22. **Michigan** is the only state touched by 4 of the 5 Great Lakes, all except Lake Ontario.
23. A few square miles of land in northern **Minnesota** produce more than 75% of our iron ore.
24. **Mississippi's** largest cash crops are, by far, cotton and soybeans.
25. Eight states border **Missouri**. What are they?
26. Fields of grain cover much of **Montana's** plains. It ranks high among the states in wheat and barley, with rye, oats, flaxseed, sugar beets, and potatoes as other important crops.

27. **Nebraska** has more miles of river than any other state.

28. **Nevada**'s Hoover Dam is the largest public works project in U.S. history. It contains enough concrete to pave a two-lane highway between New York and San Francisco.

29. **New Hampshire** has the shortest coastline of any state that touches an ocean.

30. **New Jersey** is the most crowded state in the Union, with the most people per sqare mile.

31. In **New Mexico**, the Navajo, the nation's largest Native American group, have a reservation that covers 14 million acres.

32. Giovanni Verrazano, an Italian sailing for France, found New York Bay in 1524. Henry Hudson, an Englishman sailing for the Dutch, explored the river that now bears his name, in 1609. That same year **New York** was explored, and claimed for France, by Samuel de Champlain.

33. **North Carolina**'s Outer Banks is a 200 mi. long string of narrow barrier islands off the coast. Because of the many shipwrecks which have occurred there, it is called the "Graveyard of the Atlantic".

34. **North Dakota** grows more sunflowers than any other state.

35. **Ohio** is the birthplace of 7 presidents: Grant, Hayes, Garfield, Benj. Harrison, McKinley, Taft & Harding.

36. **Oklahoma** was settled by a "land rush" in 1889. At a given signal, thousands of people on foot, in wagons and on horseback charged into what later became the state in order to claim land. Some cheated and entered early. These were called "Sooners".

37. **Oregon**'s Crater Lake is the deepest lake in the U.S. It is the caldera of an extinct volcano.

38. **Pennsylvania** is the only one of the original 13 colonies not bordered by the Atlantic Ocean.

39. **Rhode Island**, the smallest state, has the highest population density of any state but New Jersey.

40. **South Carolina**'s state tree, the saw palmetto, has such soft wood, that a fort built from its wood, actually absorbed British canon balls during a Revolutionary War battle.

41. The faces on **South Dakota**'s Mt. Rushmore are those of Washington, Jefferson, Lincoln and Theodore Roosevelt. The nearby Crazy Horse Memorial is the largest sculpture in the world, and was begun in 1948. It is, as yet, unfinished.

42. The largest earthquake in U.S. history occurred in NW **Tennessee**, instantly creating Reelfoot Lake.

43. **Texas** is the second largest state, both in size and in population.

44. **Utah**'s Great Salt Lake is 4 times as salty as any ocean on earth.

45. **Vermont** has more dairy cows per person than any other state.

46. **Virginia** is the birthplace of 8 presidents: Washington, Jefferson, Madison, Monroe, W.H. Harrison, Tyler, Taylor, and Wilson.

47. **Washington** has more glaciers than all the other 47 contiguous states combined.

48. Coal is found under half the land in the state of **West Virginia**.

49. **Wisconsin**, "The Dairy State", produces more milk than any other state.

50. **Wyoming** was the first state to give women the right to vote (1869).

THE STATES BY HEART

To memorize the states in order use the following groupings and let the rhythms of the names tell you how to recite this poem:

Alabama *(lively)*
Alaska
Arizona
Arkansas

California
Colorado
Connecticut
&
Delaware

Florida
Georgia
Hawaii
&
Idaho

Illinois
Indiana
Iowa
&
Kansas

Kentucky
Louisiana
Maine
&
Maryland

Massachusetts
Michigan
Minnesota
Mississippi *(pause)*

Missouri
Montana
Nebraska
Nevada

New Hampshire
New Jersey
New Mexico
New York

North Carolina *(slowly)*
North Dakota
Ohio(fast)
Oklahoma
Oregon
Pennsylvania

Rhode Island *(strongly)*
South Carolina
South Dakota
Tennessee

Texas(slowly)
Utah
Vermont(fast)
Virginia
Washington

West Virginia *(syllable by syllable)*
Wisconsin
&
Wyoming

Order Form

Name _____

Address _____

City _____ State _____ Zip Code _____

Email *(optional)* _____

Ship to (if different from above):

Name _____

Address _____

City _____ State _____ Zip Code _____

Email *(optional)* _____

Send check to:
LEMONTREE PRESS
P.O. Box 841
Santa Cruz, California 95061
Tel (888) 442-8998
Fax (888) 250-7350

Allow 2-3 weeks for delivery

howardschrager@lmntreepress.com
www.lmntreepress.com

RIDDLE RHYME TRILOGY TITLES	QTY	PRICE	SUBTOTAL
A Knife, and a Fork, and a Bottle, and a Cork		12.95	
Chicken in the Car and the Car Can't Go *Coming Fall 2010*		14.95	
Here's a Little Riddle for the Kids on the Block *Coming 2011*		14.95	
OTHER LEMONTREE PRESS TITLES			
LMNOP and All the Letters A to Z		18.95	
LMNOP Wall Cards		24.95	

POSTAGE & HANDLING
1-4 Books $3.50
*For 5 or more books, bulk orders, and wholesale
pricing contact LemonTree Press at:*
(888) 442-8998

Subtotal _____

Postage & Handling _____

TOTAL _____

Bound for bookstores in Fall 2010!

RIDDLE RHYME
2
TRILOGY

Chicken *in a* Car *and the* Car Can't Go
That's How You Spell Chicago

The second book of **THE RIDDLE RHYME TRILOGY** takes you deeper into the adventure of discovering the United States of America, through its great cities. Includes a short history of each city.

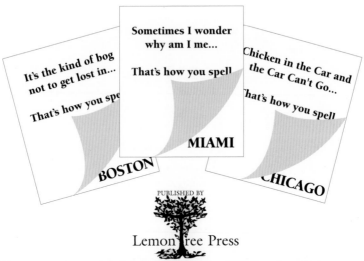

It's the kind of bog not to get lost in...

That's how you spe

BOSTON

Sometimes I wonder why am I me...

That's how you spell

MIAMI

Chicken in the Car and the Car Can't Go...

That's how you spell

CHICAGO

PUBLISHED BY

Lemon Tree Press

Bound for bookstores in 2011!

Here's *a* Little Riddle *for the* Kids *on the* Block
That's How You Spell Little Rock

The third book of THE RIDDLE RHYME TRILOGY takes you even further on your journey through the United States of America. This time from capital to capital. Includes a short history of each capital.

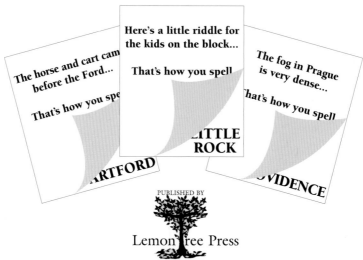

PUBLISHED BY

Lemon Tree Press